Under the
HAMMER

Under the HAMMER

The Bleeding Heart

JOSMANASCI

authorHOUSE®

AuthorHouse™ UK Ltd.
1663 Liberty Drive
Bloomington, IN 47403 USA
www.authorhouse.co.uk
Phone: 0800.197.4150

Published by AuthorHouse 06/12/2014

ISBN: 978-1-4969-8319-0 (sc)
ISBN: 978-1-4969-8318-3 (hc)
ISBN: 978-1-4969-8320-6 (e)

Foreword

Under The Hammer is a thought provoking collection of poems. An outcry of social injustice, inequality and political manipulation of African people.

In this book, José Manuel do Nascimento paints vivid pictures of what is happening in Africa, and what is also happening to Africans who flee from Africa. Which he portrays through the eyes of his country, his personal experiences and Africans in diasporas.

When justice, peace, equality, love, tolerance and political stability are **Under The Hammer**, and then gone for a penny at the expense of helpless and innocent people, it exposes how cruel life can be. The untold hardship people go through because of the selfish ambition of others.

José Manuel do Nascimento, in this book, did not only blame the African political leaders and the military juntas, but he went further to say that they are being manipulated, which he attributed to foreign powers, whose national interest motivates these political leaders and military juntas to flourish in power. Providing for their tyrannies and despotism a save haven, with red carpets to work on and black carpets to hide under.

Eventually, when these downtrodden Africans find themselves in diasporas they end up with new challenges that do not bring the best out of them, but rather challenges that take the best out of them. In some of the societies they find themselves, they are seen as beggars with choice, intruders, plunderers who come to ravage their economy and in some cases people that have primitive ways of life, and must assimilate theirs, no matter how conflicting and disastrous it is to them.

It is something unpleasant that chased the rat out of its hole. No matter how beautiful and "civilised" the rat lives out of its hole. No matter the luxury that is ravished on a caged bird, nothing can equate its precious priceless stolen freedom.

The unreserved insight that **Under The Hammer** gives to its readers is one that tells the story of oppressed Africans, and the trauma they equally go through in the lands that are supposed to soothe their hurts and nurse their injuries. José Manuel do Nascimento has cried out, who will hear his voice in this **Under The Hammer**?

Under the hammer is where we live "under for sale". It is a situation that creates tension and pressure; it is a traumatic place, and a situation of hardship, torment and psychological defeatism.

Kenechukwu Chukwunwejim
Author of "Cock Crow in Africa"

Contents

1. Why Am I Here?

It's not my own wish
That I am here
Rather the sorrow and sadness
I've gone through
I am not here by my own volition

I was born in a fertile land
Turned barren
A rich land
Turned poor
I am not here by my own volition

I am here
Because my family was murdered
My friend lost his leg
My girlfriend lost her right
I am not here by my own volition

Here I am
Learning a new language
Making new friends
Living a new freedom
Missing my beautiful land
Why am I here?

Here I am
To see my friends
Who like me escape the hammer
The hammer of human humiliation
To see my friends
Together to walk in God's will
That's why I am here

London
1992

2. If One Day I Go Back

If one day I go back
Shall pass by all ways
For long forgotten
My rebirth

If one day I go back
Shall help my country
Shall pave its streets with love
Joy shall overpower my life
New friends & old friends at my table sit

When I go back home
Shall sing a return song
Ngunga Ngele mgele Munsi zawonsono
Ngunga Ngele ngele ngele

Many tears of happiness
Victory applauses shall be in all streets
Shall visit the cemetery of my people
Shall weep by the graves of my brothers

When that day shall come
Shall say to Angola in a loud voice
"Alleluia here I am Mum"
Shall walk with all lovely mothers
Because of my message of longing
If one day I go back home . . .

Hackney London
1991

3. Freedom Faraway

Still waiting for Freedom
So far

Freedom from oppression
Of this betrayed people

Still waiting
Waiting the colourful greeting
Greeting from the sons in exile
Sons without destination

We are still waiting
Our Mum's welcome
Welcome refuses to come
Because of lies
At the podium of peacemaking

Hackney London
1993

4. Here am I

Here am I
Lost
Lost search party
Searching for the lost

Here am I
With strong desire
Desire for freedom
But, the desire has been
Chained to a wall

Here am I
Longing for hope
Which hope
Hope from oppression

Here am I
The lost without freedom

Here am I

Here am I again
Don't ask me why?

Luanda Angola
1989

5. It's Not Too Late Angola

Can't say it's too late
Because time is passing
Things are changing
Even patience
Can lose hope

I have a vision
In my innermost
Saying to me
As long as I live
There is hope

I am not too tired to live
Life is good
Life is to know how to live
I could have cried
Yet, I cry not.

What I am going through
Has got its end
Living lonely
Very lonely
Pains my heart

My pains
Have an end
My faith so strong
Like a torrent forces

I can't live without you
You are still all for me, Angola

Brixton, Oval London
1995

6. We Came Walking A Long Way

Up and down a winding way
Sun and rain
Suffering and seduction
Thirst and hunger

We came walking a long way

In multiplicity of efforts
In captivity much more
In danger of death so many times
Endless lashings

We came walking a long way

From the Jews
We received five quarantines of
Whips less one
Three times, we were lashed with sticks

We came walking a long way

Once we were stoned
Three times shipwrecked
One night and one day in the
Profundity of seas
Away from enemies
Enemies of progress

We came walking a long way

From danger of rivers
From danger of assailants
From danger of my nation
From danger of the indigenous

We came walking a long way

From danger in the city
From danger in the deserts
From danger on the sea
From danger between false brothers
From much fasting
From cold and nakedness

We came walking a long way

Instituto National de Línguas (INL), Luanda, Angola
April 1984

7. A Long Way To The Destination

One long trajectory to the destination

> Birth
> Youth
> Old age

In the long trajectory to the destination

> Up, burning sun
> Down, rain and thunder
> Persist always in the long trajectory

One long way not to turn back

> In the desert
> Hunger
> Thirst
> Illness
> Screams
> Cries

Persist always in the long trajectory

> In the green fields
> Fear
> Mines
> Bombs
> Kidnappings
> War

Persist always in the long trajectory to the destination

    In the Cities and Villages
    Corruption
    Torture
    Slander
    Illusions and separations

But persist to survive
In the long trajectory to the destination

Shoreditch, London
May 1998

8. Calm Down

Calm down
Means
Calm yourself
Calm yourself
Means
Take your time
Take your time
Means humble yourself

If the mosquito is as big
As a Tsetse-fly
You'd humble yourself

Look ahead
Means perseverance
Perseverance means
Withstanding trouble ahead
Trouble ahead
Means
The past is the only memory

If a frog is as big
As a river stone
You would look ahead.

Palanca Angola
December 1986

9. We Will Always Walk

Even though in serious illness
Even though inside the coffin
We will walk

Even under the rain
Even under the thunder
We will walk

Even in fire
Even in ashes
We will walk

Even in the burning city
We will not wait
We will walk

We will always walk
Because we are people
People of Godly devotion
Who are still dying
That is why we will always walk.

Walking away from manipulators
Who overturn our country
Made her a valley of trouble

Peckham London
January 1993

10. Leave Us Alone

What have we done?
Have we eaten your yam or coco-yam?
Leave us alone

Please leave us alone
What do we owe you?

Days and nights, shots of
Machine guns, sound of bombs
Like waves of a river

Leave our country

Please . . .

What do our ancestors owe you?
You sinners! Full of lies
In your mouths
Leave us to build our country

Please.

Hackney London
January 1993

11. That Is The Problem

That is the problem my fellow
Death of the palm nut
The deadly hammer
Has again crushed the palm nut

It has happened again my fellows

Our brothers
Our despotic bloody generals

It has happened again my fellows

You know my fellows
Cockroach is a good food for chicken

The Bakongo the cockroaches
The Generals the chickens
The chickens have eaten the cockroaches

It has happened again my fellows

Hackney London
January 1993

12. Not Happy

Walking in this world with lack of knowledge
From the beginning to the end

Not happy
To wander in this world
Like dust since the bush was set on fire

Not happy
If we leave our brothers in the darkness of this environment
Not happy
If we accept the lies of slavery
Father and mother in suffering

Where is our happiness
If our country
The country where we were born
Is still in darkness

Not happy

Hackney London
February 1992

13. Know My Name

Food available in the entire world
Death of the palm nut
Dog's feeling
Things heard by the blind
Want to tell you something friend of mine
Know my name

Death of the cricket
The pouring of rain
Happiness of the stupid
Want to tell you something friend

The voice of Ntoyo
Niunge which never crosses the border
Mbemba wherever it flies come back to its tree
Antelope which runs away from the dry season
Want to tell you something my friend
Know my name

Dreams dreamed by the dumb
Crocodile which fled from the rain
Bones to the dog
Cockroach party of cork
Want to tell you something my friend
Know my name

How would you know it?
My friend
My name is Mayindu
Know it today.
My name shall be Mayindu
Until Angola
Until Africa
Know Luvuvamu

Detention Centre, Heathrow Terminal 3, London
October 1989

14. A Big Bang

A BANG, A big noiseless bang
A bang on my family
Apart everything everybody fall
Wall of separation
Which torments us
Crushes our high spirit
Plucks our peace
Firmly attached on the peaceful tree

Children manipulated
Imprisoned against parents
Parents' innocence unheard
Limited visitation
Which string is pulled
By a godless hand

Our Fate we know
Ultimately in Heaven's Hand
Thus, solidly we stand
Until
They come back home
And we shall sit together again
To smile in the sun shine

Hackney, London
une 2006

15. Whom Shall I Tell?

Whom shall I tell?
I look ahead
And look behind
Nobody
Whom shall I tell?

Whom shall I tell?
No mother in the kitchen
To ditch me food like
Other children whose plates are laden with food
My eyes are wide

Whom shall I tell?
When I speak
Voice unheard
When I speak
They call me Ntoyo the bird
Bearer of bad message
Go back where you come from

Whom shall I tell?
Ghost bat
Lack of family
No-one will weep
The day I die

Whom shall I tell?
Frog in the river
Owl in the forest
Wandering all alone

Dedicated To:
Luisa Sebastião
Miranda House, Shoreditch, London
1993

16. Dog Feelings

If we knew how to talk
And speak

Hum, if we had been chosen
To speak
To do so would be joyful

If speaking was speech
As we have been taught
We would do so

Thank you for talking
Without knowing how to speak

Thank you
You all my brothers
Enslaved
You mouth sealed
One day you shall talk

When your mouth unsealed
My brothers!
Talk!

Barton Close, Hackney, London
1990

17. Laugh

Lack of knowledge
They laugh
Lack of discernment
They laugh
Lack of understanding
They laugh
But if you are laughing don't fall yourself

Is it for lack of material possession?
They laugh at you
Lack of knowledge
They're laughing
If it is for persistence in education
They're still laughing
If it is for lack of intelligence
They called you stupid
Their words lack understanding

Laughing without knowledge
Laugh for nothing
Don't laugh at me you ridiculer
Because I am still living
You can laugh now
But
The future shall surely laugh at you

Bungo, Uíge
1976

18. Sorrows

Want to tell you something
Don't let me die
Land so barren
No freedom

Want to tell you
The sad condition
All bodies fired
Without water and blood

Have told everybody
But no one helped
The land was mined
People tortured

Life full of sorrow
Want to tell somebody
Who will care for my land and my people
Who will give them water and life

Cambrige
1993

19. The Truth

This is the voice
Cannot be changed
This is the truth
Cannot be a liar
The truth is truth

Like this you obliged us
In 1961
Like this you betrayed us
In 1975
Like this you persecuted us
In 1993
The truth is truth

We weep like that
Don't oblige us your manner
We walk like that
Don't want to decay
The truth is truth

We don't want to be like you
Don't oblige us to be corrupt
We don't want to eat your food
Only our mwamba
The menu of Africanism

Don't force us to speak your language
We don't want to be assimilated
To lose our roots
The truth is truth

"31 de Janeiro", Nsoso, Angola
16 January 1987

20. No More

I am stubborn
I am unshakeable
Stubborn and unshakeable
To human humiliation

For decades and centuries
Humiliation flourished like sunny flowers
But my foot is planted deep down
Into the concrete earth
No more!

My weary bones
My hurting heart
Have said no more
To the whip
That showed me
Where I belong

I am stubborn
I am unshakeable
No longer submissive
To human humiliation
Who wants to know
Let him know
No more!

Instituto National de Línguas (INL), Luanda, Angola
1984

21. Mama

There is my mama
Black and so beautiful
Endowed with rich jewels
That's my mama
Oh! Mama my mama
You are lovely

Mama, your seeds sail away
Got drunk on
English wine
Got fat on American burgers
Got bewitched by Asian fruits
Lost all lost

Mama, sweet mama
How can they find the way back?
They long for your warm embrace
A nostalgic embrace
Full of memories

Your stream sides
The little brooks flow
Down from the mountain
Your fertile farms
That can make even stones grown
Your beautiful birds
That sings songs
And heals sad hearts

Mama, Oh! Mama
How can we forget you?
Can bear to forget you
My mama Africa

Institut Karl Marx, Makarengo, Luanda, Angola
1985

22. If the world offered them the Truth

Want to forget the flowers of seasons passed?
Hundreds upon hundreds of years
Missions of these flowers
Blossom and blossom
I reached out my hand
Chose one
One in the middle
Shining like the crisp of the sun in the East
Sit tight on your thinking stool
Think of flowers this season
Oh! A shame, unspeakable shame
Each flower at one another's throat

Can you fore-see
State of coming flowers?
No fertile ground for them to grow
As they must have destroyed
Their own world by their own fingers
As just for the reason
The world stole the truth from them

Instituto National de Línguas (INL), Luanda, Angola
1985

23. The Boot

The boot should have
Stood unmoved and unruffled
Should not have
Taken the sudden flight
So says the major

Maybe I was stupid
Giving you my time
Should not have let you
Call me a donkey
Should not have given you
Such opportunity to call me names

All the triggers my fingers pulled
All the brothers' blood
That flows from my gun
Yet! You call me
Stupid!
Donkey!
Wait then!
You will see

Planalto Central, Huambo, Angola
1981

24. The Old House

In my dream
Our old house
Three small rooms and a lounge
The lounge
Where smoke made it's paradise

In our old house
The twins were born
And so my first handwriting
Where mother's hand
Caressed my skin

In our old house
At the end of the road
At Mbongi a mfinda
The place of four palm trees
Where I shared a bed with my friend
Judas the puppy
Famous for its friendliness
Notorious for its tricks

In my dream
I am an alien
In our old house
I wait, I long for
The day, the moment
I shall set foot
In our old house
Which lives in me
In my dream

Hackney, London
1991

25. Don't want to be Rich?

Who should want to be rich?
Not me! My brother
Father and Mother were poor
So happy they were
In poverty I grew

If you offer me a damp house
I'll accept
I have been living in it
When friends come visiting
I'll not be ashamed to receive them

Don't want to be rich?
I've got two hands
I've got two feet
I've got two eyes
And a head
They're not lost
I can live well on them
That's why I don't want to be rich

If you love me
Love also my poverty
The day my poverty ends
The world ends
Anyone who loves you
In your poverty
Truly loves you
Rosa do Golfe

Instituto National de Línguas (INL), Luanda, Angola
1983

26. Momento de Partida

When the twilight comes
Never drop any tears
Never say nothing for nothing happened
Except
Momento de Partida has come

The dawn of transition
Goodbye might be
Too heavy to say
Shining that was there
When I was there
Might go to embrace darkness
As it will be
Momento de Partida

When it comes
Like a sudden rush
Be careful to remember
All my recommendations

Miranda House, Shoreditch, London
1999

27. Stop Intimidating

I was born to be a man
To speak as a man
To look seriously as a man
Stop intimidating

In the spirit
My heart
My mind
My hands
My feet
Stand firm as a man

Your whip of intimidation
Only my flesh can touch
Your looks of intimidation
Only shall trigger off
My manly stubbornness

I was born a man
I shall act as a man
When I speak
It will mock your intimidation
I am a man
Your intimidation can't stop me
Until your intimidation stops

Hackney, London
November 2007

28. Who knows me

Who am I
Who I was
Who I'll be
They don't know me
I speak to the people of this world
Together with different words
In sorrow and happiness
But they still do not know me

How am I
How I was
How I'll be
For all I do and teach
In my talk and walk
In reunions and assemblies
But they still do not know me

Harvey House, Shoreditch, London
2000

29. Under Arrest

Word of misery
Word never forgotten
A disaster word
Of under arrest
You under arrest

No sense
In cell isolated
Cup of black coffee?
Thank you, innocent voice
God bless you
White coffee
Under arrest

My son
Will never forget
You under arrest
I came here sir
To arrest you
Who sent you?
My colleagues!
You under arrest

Sometimes no sense
The under arrest
A chicken
Under arrest

Hackney, London
ay 2007

30. War

Lies flourish like watered green grasses
Passion of hatred
In every heart
War delinquents insult peace moves
Slander and propaganda
Cold hands of mischief and destruction

As men in love with hatred
Release arrows of destruction
Million voices silenced
Graven desires gratified

The terrible tales of war
Are but a sad song to sing
War has driven peace to hell
Built a chaotic disastrous heaven
Where pain and sorrow
Flow like ZAMBEZY RIVER

London
1992

31. The Telephone Conversation

The telephone goes again
Again and again
Never ever tired
Ingue! Darling Ingue!
Are you at the airport?

No! Paul, no! Darling Paul!
My flight definitely
Thursday unfailingly Thursday

Sure?
Ingue are you sure this time?

Never been sure in my life
Am as sure as sure can be

Oh! Ingue! Darling Ingue
can wait to see

Again and again
Never ever tired
Knock on our door

Ingue is coming
Coming this time
Her flight in three thirty Thursday
She promised
She swore
She is so sure

Anxiously we wait
Our welcoming gifts
By our sides
Roses of hope
Roses for Ingue
By our sides
She promised to arrive today

The telephone goes again
Again and again
Never ever tired

Ingue! Where are you?
Angola! Darling Paul!
Coming on Tuesday
Unfailingly Tuesday

This never ever ending
Circle of promise
That has killed
Our roses a dozen times
Left the love sick heart
Devastated

Flight landed
Here we go, Ingue
Arrived

Barton Close, Hackney, London
1990

32. Secret Love (V)

Hidden love cannot be told
Hearts that beat as one
Cannot hide secrets
Am I a coward?
My heart cannot express my affection

Her shining black skin perfumed
I call it, Eu Gosto . . .
That makes my heart to beat
Like a Conga drum

Her attractive eyes
Pierce the deep darkness
Like a torch light
Humiliating the darkness

Hidden love cannot be told
There is love in my heart
I cannot express
Cannot go to the garden
The beauty of the garden
Its colourful flowers
Its natural beauty

A heavy memory
Of your untapped untouched beauty
Which makes my heart beat
Like a Conga drum

My secret love
Hidden in my heart
Scared to unveil
If unrequited

Kilburn, London 1994

The Bleeding heart

Contents

1. Immaculate

Pure and gentle
Calm and sweet
Are his sleep
Innocent eyes
Mark of his purity

His little angelic smile
His delicate skin made of wool
His little fragile hand not bloodstained
His touching sound of cry
From Alpha to Omega
From beginning to the end
All about him
Are pure and immaculate

This stainless heart
This hallowed creature
Knows no guile
Hatred and wickedness of this world
A stranger to him
When you see a baby
You see how innocent
This world needs to be

2. Love Apart

So beautiful
So loving
Like morning flower
So her beauty
Her irresistible beauty
That makes my heart beat faster
Like a loud African drum
So is my heart before her
Lost in her beauty

Her love for me is untold
So deep is her love
But there's a big gulf
In between us
The difference of our colours

The mulata with cat eyes
With hair flowing from her head
To her heels
Like a wedding gown
From first class parents
Who tread on money
And bath in wine
Daughter of a white colonialist

Me! A common African
Son of a farmer
A friend of the forest
Deeply scared

As attractive as a diamond
Blows my blood hot with love
My struggle with black charming girls
Who loved me
Did not give up on me
But intoxicated by Lizia

The beautiful mulata
Who breaks my heart
Whose terrible blow
Cripples my heart
The sacred heart
That is in love

3. Parting

When I my mum's womb left
The first friend I made was mum's hand
Which lifted up to suck
Nourishment from her black breast

Now nature empowered with manhood
Walks, watches and marches out
With the most powerful
On a mission for the country

Combating enemies day by day
As hands get together in unity
To form a strong force
Manoeuvring terror day by day

As the sound of danger ended
Our mission ended
Homeward we march
Happiness hovers round our heads
We sing and whistle
Our joyous songs towards
Where we came from

Children and women
Line up on the street to cheer
While weak men in bushes hide
For shame

In our mind
As we came to our mission end
Parting from one another
Is a sweet bitter burden

Huambo, Angola 23rd March 1983

4. Dieu est mon droit

At the tribunal court room
Eyes of man and woman
Roll down in tears
Eyes in despair look
Like one who's lost a loved one

Weary feet conquered
By constant climbing of stairs
Court staircase
The bottled up feeling
An inexpressible anguish

At the tribunal court room
Mind in constant trouble
Condemnation or liberty
Questions begin
Are you Mrs or Miss
Question after question

Unknowingly
At the high top
Where the judge sits
Are written words
Proclamation of innocence
If innocent
Proclamation of condemnation
If guilty
Two faced words

Look what is written there
Proclaims the highest
"GOD IS MY RIGHT"
Be not afraid
The words are for you
My innocent one

King Eduards Road
30the July 2007

5. In Search

The bag of Joblessness
Is heavy, too heavy to carry

From one Job Centre
To another
In search of Job

From one point
To another
In search of Job

From one newspaper
To another
In search of Job

Gaze at every Job, any Job
No chance

When newly finding above
Life a struggle
Language a barrier
Intellectualism looks down

When your arch-enemy
Unemployment follows you around
Daily bread a misfortune
Which unearth nostalgia
Your home sweet home
Forced under pressure to abandon
To crunch under
The heavy weight of unemployment

Hackney, London 31st December 2007

6. Don't Really Understand

So why?
Why us?
From where?
Till when?
Will it continue
Do not really know
Do not really understand

No one does
Tribes against tribes
Pointing accusing fingers
At one another

Why all these?
Why just my continent
War! War! and bloodshed
Till when?

People running, weeping
Only the invisible heavenly one
Knows and understands

7. The Abandoned

Look at my palms
What do you see?
My past
My present
My future
Look at my palms
A hand that shakes misery

Look into my eyes
What do you see?
My tears
My vision
My looks
Look into my eyes
The short and long walk

Look into my heart
What do you see?
The secret
The lamentations
The beats
Look into my heart
The fast pumping heart

Look at my black lips
Slave of bad and good kisses
And look at my footsteps
Tremendous in the narrow road
Look at my footsteps
In the timid mines infested land

Hackney, London
1990

8. Bureaucracy

Sits in office
List of programmes
Tasks and targets in vain
Contemporary world
In bureaucracy based

Decayed countries
With lots of compromised
Manipulated people
So many untrue words
Desk full of false proposal papers
Made to be by bureaucracy

Approving war project
Accepting killing and marring
Brainwashed by colonialism
Accomplishes unknown project
Based in bureaucracy

Bureaucracy provokes laziness
Laziness provokes neglect
Neglect provokes bad administration
Bad administration enemy of progress
Which kills the goals
All because of bureaucracy

9. Remote Control

Little but powerful
Endowed with power
To change
To manipulate

Like remote controlled objects
So are our leaders
In the hands of
Neo-colonial Lords
Who turn them left and right
Like Zombies they follow

Follow courses not for their people
Courses that leave their people
At one another's throats
Which were offered them
For a sit-tight King
Remote controlled
By neo-colonial Lords

Who see nothing good
In the African agenda
But their remote control
Goes for anything
Which cheers their heart
And
Refills their treasury

10. Museum of Slavery

It was here
First saw chilling shocking
Horror of Human Humiliation
Infamous house
Which parades the foot-print
Of slavery
Built in the protesting beach
Inside the illustration
This illegal commerce

It was here
Priceless brothers sold
Without a price
Without a struggle
Without a voice

Forced Atlantic journey
Known unknown destination
Black brothers burden
whose faces weep under the whip
Forced ship of despair
The triangular trade

It was here
Saw historic house
House of sad memories
Man, wife and children
Shipped off sorrowfully
Many died not arriving
Many died on gilbet
Whipped endlessly

It was here
Africa was plundered
Her Kingdom ravaged
Here!
The Coast of Africa
Truth betrayed
Truth was sold
For a penny
Black brothers
African brothers
Neglected and taken for curs

11. Granting Permission in Fear

From here to there
Then
From there to here
Our cocoa comes as chocolate
Our palm kernel becomes body lotion
Our fresh food canned poison
Back to US

Healthy food turns unhealthy
The canned food that runs stomachs
Our bright faces turn pale
As sickness becomes our companion

Now we are called the dead continent
Continent of diseases
Continent of monkeys
From where came the diseases?

Now we are seen as
New planet of conflict
Conflict of problems
We know nothing of
We set the fire of conflict?
As we are afraid to say no
The mothers want our permission
Permission to do what?
Permission she already took by force

12. Decolonizing the mind

From village to village
From town to town
From one part to another part
Everywhere loses their native names
At most mutilated native names

Everything African fake
Everything African primitive
Every negative thing undesirable
To our ignorance
We gave a nod
To their everything
Their every nonsense

They bomb our brains
With colonized concepts
The right owners
Find false owners
Our minds upside down turn
Our left and our right lost
We went in all directions
To no direction
Our colonized minds confused
Who will decolonise
These brainwashed Africans?

13. Nature has lost its hold on women

Want to see
Your natural beauty
Put aside
Your make-up
Show us what nature
Has done with you

Put aside
Your nail-polisher
Your lipstick
Your bleaching cream
Your wig
Your eye shadow
All your make-up
Put aside

Then
Parade your beauty
Let us see
Nature has lost
Its hold on women
None: indeed none
Has been faithful to nature
They have all gone crazy
Crazy over artificial
And made nature
A lonely orphan

14. Mosquito

All its life
A trouble-maker
No-one can forget
Your dreadful trouble
Buzzing present
That makes everyone alert
That irritating unwelcome sound
That makes men fight with the air
Clapping in the air
To no-one

You tiny thing
Mischievous small thing
Flying in mid-air
Harmlessly harmful

Ambitious for your
Rich sweet reddish drink
Yet,
Red is danger
Fearless mosquito
Terrorising even giants

Its troublesome sound
Keeps everyone sleepless
Its bite
Keeps everyone sick
Mosquito the smallish troubler

José Manuel do Nascimento
Well Street, Hackney, London
8th March 1990

15. Where were you that early morning?

That early morning
Where went you?
Searched
The house, the street
All over the place
No sight of you
Where were you
That early morning?

You and our counsellor
Where went you?
Somewhere in the city
Knows both of you
Together are
Waited for you
To see me off
To the airport
You were nowhere
To be found
Where were you
That early morning?

On my way to the airport
My heart longed
To see you
At the airport
Before my departure
My eyes went
To and fro
Here and there
In search of you
Longing for your
Goodbye and kisses
Your assuring smiles
But!
Nowhere to see you
Where were you
That early morning?

José M. do Nascimento
Well Street, Hackney, London 12th October 1989

16. The Past

Moonlight smiles at night
As I sat at a quiet corner of the night
Thinking
Thinking of love
Consumed by love
Love steals my time

Sleeping in silence
All the chances
The world offered me
To accomplish my love life
Yet sleeping in silence
Never made use of the chances
Oh! She is lovely, so lovely

As my soul mourns
Lost my chances
The thought torments
My soul
As her beauty
Her happy face
Her lovely voice
Echoes on my ears
The thought of the past
Torments me

17. Love is not unpair

Everything is in pairs
Everything comes and goes in pairs
Caring
Is caring for you
Craziness in life
Is craziness for you
Love is not unpair

Whatever one says
Is said to or for someone
Gifts are given by someone
To somebody
Love is not unpair

What was created
Was created in pairs
The eyes
Bad and good
Cause and motive
Front and back
Death and life
Love is not unpair

18. Foretell

Want to foretell
How the world will be
When darkness comes
Darkness of man's wickedness to man
Everyman's heart a stone
Death and sorrow in every corner
As men will build walls over their hearts

No man can reach his fellow
The sky will turn blood
In protest
The earth will turn red
Having gotten drunk
Too much blood

Every land
Shall be fields of anguish
Bright souls
Shall have their light extinguished
Every beautiful land
A graveyard

If the world keeps
On its present path
This I foretell

19. Heat of Love Music

Early this morning
When a new day begins
Eyes open
With strong thoughts
Wallowing in my heart
As the heat of love music
Plays heavily in my heart

Silently sitting in a corner
Not dreaming
Not resting
But listening
Listening to your love music
Its heat refuses to settle
Until I
See your beautiful face
My gorgeous princess
Until I
Feel your sweet embrace
Until
Your smiles beyond

Thinking of you has kept me going
In this land
Covered by pure white
The down pour enemy

Isolation
Has taught me
How to love you more
Isolation of conspiracy
My gorgeous princess
The heat of your love music
Keeps me going

José M. do Nascimento
Miranda House, Hoxton, London 21st January 1991

20. Snow in my heart

Now
I walk the white streets
The cold white streets
Snow in my hand
As cold as ice cubes
Chills my blood

In far away
Sunny sweet home
Where birds fly happily
In mid-air
Dogs and cats
Walk in pairs
Trees wave happily
To the passing wind

The noisy lorry
Over-flowing with passengers
Again and again
Can see
Kisangi kya mongue
Mysterious forest
Noisy kingdom of animals
Longing for my land
As these cold white streets
Crush my bones
Snow in my hand
Chills my blood
Is it possible to see my land?

Miranda House, Hoxton, London 7th February 1991

21. My life

Who can help?
Who can help this poor soul?
Who wanders off from self?
Whose life is as cold as ice
Who mysterious life
Is tormented by dreams

Ugly dreams of ugly things
Every night sleep
Runs far away from him
He call
He cries

No-one to help
In the strange land
He finds himself
Exiled from himself

Who can help him?
Find himself

Everywhere
Everything
Everybody
Strange so strange
He calls
He cries
For help
Who can help?

Man of Inspiration

Content

Birthday, badday

Before I was born
He gave me eighty years
To live
Birthday badday
And
Everyone's good day
They laugh, and dance

Don't laugh
I am not happy
Birthday badday
Each birthday nearer
My grave I draw
As each year
Leaves me with less

Josmanaci
King Edwards's rd
Hackney London 14/07/08

Hope a smile

Hope gives smile
Smile gives happiness
Life nothing without
Hope

She gives smile
Longates our life
Live with hope
Talk with hope
Sing with hope
Watch with hope
Wait with hope

She gives us
Reason to smile
Imagine if the world
Has hope
How wonderful if will be
Man and wife together
Brothers and sisters together
All smiling
Just because of hope

Josmanaci
King Edwards's rd
Hackney London 10/8/08

Insomnia

Difficulties
Pains
Grief's and sorrows
Accompany me to bed
Heavy spirit
Over-weighs my sleep
My eyes wide awake
As sleep allude me

Gloomy faces
Violence and death
Cries of helpless villagers
Caught in needless foolish war
Torment my sleep
Insomnia my midnight enemy

Families tore apart
Faces made hungry by war
March through my weary street
Torment my sleep
Invoke insomnia

Josmanaci
Harvey house, Colville estate
London, shoreditch 13/03/1993

Man of inspiration

Nearby a man
Walks in inspiration
Mind deep in thought
Meaningless things meaningful

Nearby a man
Stops to think
Finds everything everywhere
Interesting

Nearby a man
Walks into the garden
His lights up
As smiles of inspiration
Decorates his face
Like the flowers
Decorates the garden
Man of inspiration
The poet

Josmanaei
Victoria Park, hackney
London 22/05/08

Nothing, something

Crocodile out of the river
Is nothing
Crocodile in the river
Is something
The river it's domain
Where it's power and strength
Over powers its prey

Crocodile flees from rain
Yet is empowered by the river
Crocodile weak in lands
Dangerous in the river
Its home
Where it is something

        Josmanaci
        Dorset Street, Baker Street
        London 12/4/07

Katanganika

Ageless Katanganika
Ancient!
Flows from ages to ages
Who told you?
We can't cross
Who told you?
We can't fish
Who told you?
We can't swim
In our great Katanganika

Ancient Katanganika
Burundi your domain
Your sweet sound
Invoke our childhood memory
At your ageless torrent
Where
We fish, swim and wash
Our little selves!
Katanganika!
You flow in pride

Josmanaci
King Edwards's rd
7/05/08

Igwe

London knows no other
But,
Queen alone
Every royalty
Unknown in London Street
Igwe
Born in Mbongi a mfinda

As the Igwe
Lost his crown
To London
Who know no other?
But the queen

Royalty a cleaner
The cleaner
The Igwe
Who lost his crown?
In the crowdy London

Josmanaci
Central London, holbon
27/08/08

The threat

One day
This small tongue
Shall cease from speaking
It's voice never shall be heard
As the revolutionaries
Parade their false intention
Afraid of the truth

One day
This small tongue of truth
Shall never speak
As the revolutionaries
Parade the machine gun
And seals the tongue
The only tongue
Who dare speak truth

One day
The wicked secret gun
Shall be heard
Forever seal the tongue
And truth shall
Never be heard

Josmanasci
Hackney Well Street
15/09/08

Nasci-Vive-Morera'

First time eyes open
It was in Africa
My birth place
In my mothers black hands
Of rose flowers
It fragrances enrich my nose

In Africa lives
Hunting down the hunter
In the thick forest of Africa
Where streams empty
Itself in the endless sea
In a strange land lives
But my spirit and soul
Live in Africa

In Africa
My tired bone

      Josmanasci
      Shall rest London 19/10/1995
      When my ancestor
      Join

MESSANGER FROM ABOVE

Everyday
When I look at the sky
Someone is there

Everyday
When I look at the sky
Someone touches my heart

When I look at myself
I am alone but not alone
All my troubles on my head
Yet someone is carrying them

Everyday
In my garden
He ministers to me
Vanda, son! Vanda

When I seat down
He touches all my bruises and troubles
With love unimaginable
Will he ascend?
Heaven today?

Vanda

JOSMANASCI
King Edward's Rd
13/03/09 3.00 AM

SOON

Long time no see
My beloved
Such a long time
Waiting patiently
For opportunity to free me

To fulfill
My plans for you
Am coming very soon
We are coming
As you're warm
Embrace awaits us
We will soon come comes home

JOSMANASCI
King Edward's Rd

13/03/09

LOVE

Love is a fire
Set heart ablaze
Unimaginable fire
Life is in his bosoms

Love is a fire
Unstoppable
She sets sorrow ablaze
And gives birth to happiness
She sets misery ablaze
And gives birth to joy

Love is a fire
She sets hopelessness ablaze
And gives birth to hope
She sets doubt ablaze
And gives birth to confidence

Yes!
Love is a fire

JOSMANASCI
King E dwards Rd
E9 7SF 13/03/09

ALWAYS LAUGH

He laughs always
This man always laughs
In the streets
To strangers
He always laughs
Everywhere every time

Content of his spirit
Reflects in his laughter
He drown his misery
In his laughter
He is an alien
To sorrow and sadness

He laughs always
His laughter does not
Depict that he is
Rich or poor

But
A reflection of his spirit
This laughs always
To attract goodness

JOSMANASCI
King Edward's Rd

KALUDIDIKO

Don't cry, my son
Don't cry, my daughter
Shall be back
Back on time
When you need me
I will there

Don't cry

Your suitcase
Yours, truly, clothes
Yours, truly, Shoes
Say farewell to friends
Don't cry, my children
Kaludidiko
I am taking you
Back home

JOSMANASCI
King Edward's Rd
31/03/09 4.45Am

LEAVE ME ALONE

My weary body
Yearns
Says, "Leave me alone"
As over-whelming troubles
Over flow like river
Sub due my people
On my door
Every hand knocks
At my door
Every feet step

Their troubles too heavy
For me alone to crack
My weary body
Says, "Leave me alone"
My soul softer by care
Says, "What must be done
Must be done

JOSMANASCI
King Edward's Rd
11/03/09 E9 7SF

LONELY

Walking down lonely street
This lonely man
Mouth nipped but lack of language
No one to talk to
As every one their language

At the shops
At the bus stops
At the streets
No word to express himself
Lonely simple men
All to himself

Loneliness haunts him
Stomach empty
Loneliness failed him
No language, no word

Isolated in the room
Thinking drifts him after
Dead or alive family
Know not
Crying and insomnia
Kept him awake all night

Across the ocean
At other side
Loneliness consume
But thought
Thought of family
Live and wait
Eagerly for reunion

JOSMANASCI
King Edward's Rd, E9 7SF
06/04/09

Five thousand kilometers

Whenever we want to go
We will go
Don't follow us
You are an intruder
A lying persecutor

There is no good
In you
Heaven will make you
Run five thousand kilometers
Five thousand kilometers behind us

And we shall sail smoothly
Smoothly to our destination
Without you disguised help

We are strong willed

Don't forget
Heaven will make
You walk five thousand kilometers
Five thousand kilometers behind us

JOSMANASCI
King Edward's Rd
06/04/09 E9 7SF

The River

The day was raining
Went to the river
Saw a flowing water
Clean water but, dangerous to swim
Scare of me.
Invoke my childhood memory
Sadly, hear mysterious voice
Don't worry, you can manage
Jump in and swim.
The tormentor of life Kimbombo.
Did I do so.

Twenty four hours heavy raining
Went back to the river
Saw a strong flowing water
Very, very dirty water and dangerous
Full of woods, small trees and glasses
No mysterious heard
The sound of Kimbombo disappear
No way
No longer manipulated
Kimbombo, stop.

One good day
At riverside flowing slowly
Saw a clean water
Thinking not danger at all
But dangerous swimming indeed
Again heard Kimbombo voice
Swim, swim
Attempted to jump in
Danger came
But escape out of danger.

Unimaginable death
Of intruder Kimbombo
The tricks of Kimbombo
Kimbombo, there will be more jump
No more attempt to swim
Kimbombo as you flow, find your way

Josmanasci
2 Oswald Street
Clapton
London E5 OBT
29/01/2010

Capuqueiros

Shouts
A startle and a scream in the air
Gosh, what going on?

The laughter of funniest jokers
Whose brown tinted teeth
Handwork of years cola nuts
Mar their drunken smiles
Gosh, what's the shout?

Adventure
Adventure of glasses of Capuca
Gosh, what kind of Capuca is this?
That has made their brains annoyed
Annoyed whit normality

Gosh, where are they going?
Invitation of Capuca
Is no good for the brain and the pocket
This Capuca a strong spirit
Shall definitely demonize their brains.

Josmanasci
Nelito Soares Rua
C8 Luanda–Angola
1979

Prisoners

Living without freedom
      Without peace
      Without victory
      Without memory
We are prisoners

Living without calm
      With the hurt heart
      Without tranquility
      Without fix place
We are prisoners

Living out of our Lands
      Without volation
      Without happiness
      Without conscientiousness
We are really prisoners of conscience

                Jomanasci
                Immigration Court Room
                Temple-London
                December/1990

Glossary

Ngunga ngele ngele muna nsi zazonsono, ngunga ngele ngele ngele
The bell is playing over the world, the bell is paying.

Bakongo . . . . People born in north of Angola{
Kongo Kingdom}
Ntoyo . . . . Kind of little mysterious bird
Niunge . . . . Litle rat who never cross the road
Mbemba . . . . Big bird, wherever his flys, always back
in his original tree
Mayindu . . . . Clumsy or disastered
Luvuvamu . . . . Peace
Mwamba . . . . Nuts African soup
Mbongi a mfinda . . . . Flores city, name of the village where
the author was born
Situated in Wandu-Mucaba-Uige.
Momento de partida. . . . . The time of departure
Rosa do golf . . . . Name of the girl in golf-Luanda
Capuqeiros. . . . . Drunkers of Capuca
Capuca . . . . A strong drink spirit made whith
maize, banana mixed whith
1 Sugar{ we call it African wisky}
Kimbombo . . . . A strong drink made whith flour
powder and sugar
Ingue. . . . . Name of person
Gilbelt . . . . A metallic instrument used in past to
punish slaves till to Die
Eu gusto . . . . I like it
Igue. . . . . The King, in native language of
Nigeria{ Yuruba}
Kaludidiko. . . . . Don't you cry
Nasci-Vive-Morera' . . . . Born-Leave-Will die
Katanganika. . . . . Name of well know in Africa history
Kissangi kia monge . . . . Name of one the mysterious forest in
Wandu-Mucaba-Uige,
{the water of his river is very cold like
ice, when you get in
That forest only take one thing no
more than two, fruit,
Animal, fish, any another thing. If you
do so . . .

Biography

Jose' Manuel do Nascimeto{ Josmanasci } born in Mbongi a mfinda, Wandu-Mucaba, province Uige-Angola, fled the country at the time of conflict and civil war to U.K. Graduate in Phisolophy and mission studies at International Bible Institute in London { 11/11/1996 }.

He has been merited and given a medal as first writer in exile of his Community of Angolan Association Refuge and Organisation in U.K. {OCARU} with he's the co-found, his first book MUNGUNDA ZA N'TMA AME { IN MY INNEMOST}, in the year, the Anglican Church released through USPG a album of Banyongo music called VOICES FROM ANGOLA where he was a singer with his fellow five Angolans in mean time the Human Manority Right Group published a book which the same title VOICES FROM ANGOLA, which his active participation.

At 50 Anniverssary of United Nations at Westminister Methodist Hall he was there to represent Angola, Congo and Gabon gospel with his group The Seraph Choir he founded in 1992, He coursed at Oxford University Queen Elizabeth the course the forced immigrant through Human Right Watch, Worked as volunteer in different project in the Muscum of London {Drama in the Docks and inspiration in the picture}, Museum in Docklands and Barbican Museum.

Before leaving Angola, He studied Linguistics and Translation in National Institute of National Languages where he gained his Diploma and worked in. After his military service in Dalatando And Huambo as Calculador do BM21, back to Luanda in the Institute working, then one year Went to work at Assembleia do Povo today National Assembly as the Kikongo first translator Where he was in charge to translate law book and different papers in Information Department And Translation also student of Journalism in Institute of Karl-Marx Makarengo.